Field Guide to the Irish Music Session was originally published in 1999 by Roberts Rinehart Publishers. Unfortunately, not long afterward, that firm found itself mired in legal troubles (unrelated—not my fault!), and the fallout affected *Field Guide*. As a result, the book's life ended up far more complicated and, ultimately, shorter than it should have been.

In the years since it went out of print, people have inquired about *Field Guide* from time to time, and it still gets the occasional mention in Irish music circles. The fact that it hasn't been forgotten has often made me wish there were a manageable, economical means of making the book available again.

Enter the miracle of print-on-demand publishing. Having gone through the process of publishing my book *The Devil's Food Dictionary: A Pioneering Culinary Reference Work Consisting Entirely of Lies* by the POD method this year, I realized I could use the same approach to resurrect *Field Guide to the Irish Music Session*. I'm happy to say you are holding the result in your hands.

The opportunity to reprint the book of course offered the chance to revise it, but I decided to resist that temptation. Apart from a new binding (now paperback) and this preface, all content is identical to that of the 1999 version. This means that any statements I may have had second thoughts about since writing the book remain, for better or worse, unchanged. Furthermore, a couple of typographical irregularities that sneaked into the original edition persist into this one. But I can live with that; I hope you can too. If nothing else, it allows us to point to at least one thing about Irish traditional music that has not changed in the past ten years.

I take a lot of pleasure in being able to revive *Field Guide to the Irish Music Session*, but it's an occasion of some sadness as well. My dear friend Rob Adams, the book's illustrator, died a couple of years after the book's birth, and I regret that he's not around to see his quirky drawings return to bookstore shelves. I dedicate this new edition to him. For both of our sakes, I hope you find it worthwhile.

—BARRY FOY
Seattle, August 2008

praise for

FIELD GUIDE TO THE
irish music session

Very funny, very amusing.
—Seamus Connolly,
Director of Music, Song, and Dance for Irish Studies,
Boston College

You need never again tread the delicate ground of explaining
to a fellow musician how you think he or she is obstructing
the session; instead offer them this book as a gift. For those
who are unsure of the generally accepted ground rules for
participating in a session, this is essential reading.
—Martin Hayes, internationally known fiddler

FIELD GUIDE TO THE
irish
music
session

BARRY FOY

drawings by Rob Adams

FROGCHART PRESS
SEATTLE

Frogchart Press, Seattle
Box 85095
Seattle, WA 98145-1095, USA
www.frogchartpress.com

ISBN 978-0-9817590-1-2
Library of Congress Control Number: 2008907429

Field Guide to the Irish Music Session was originally published in a hardback edition by Roberts Rinehart Publishers in 1999 (original ISBN 1-57098-241-4).

Contents

AUTHOR'S NOTE

The author takes complete and sole credit for the excellence of the text of this book; critiques by fiddlers Paul Michel and Conor Byrne and guitarist Peter Gilmore, as well as discussions with those gentlemen on the subjects of sessions and Irish music in general, were of no help at all. Nor does he wish to express his gratitude to L. E. McCullough and Armin Barnett for taking him to his first Irish sessions and generally grounding him in this music. The truth is, he could have done without it.

As for the wonderful drawings, the selection of art dealer, musician, and philosopher Rob Adams as this book's illustrator called for impeccable taste and first-rate judgment. The author pleads guilty to both. Rob would have been the first choice even if he had asked to be paid.

—BARRY FOY

introduction

WHY THIS BOOK WAS WRITTEN,

WHO SHOULD READ IT,

AND WHO NEEDN'T BOTHER

If you live in Ireland, the notion of a book on the nature of traditional music sessions is bound to seem ridiculous. What, you'll ask, could all this codifying, itemizing, and prescribing possibly have to do with something as spontaneous and self-regulating as a *seisiún*?

The same may hold true for natives of the Irish enclaves of London, say, or New York or Boston, cities where the music has been handed down generation by generation and where the particulars of session etiquette, as well as a basic understanding of the point of it all, are a matter of general consensus and need no explaining.

But what about the rest of us, those who may live at some remove from the epicenters of Irish music? Alas, for us the situation is more complex.

It's a painfully familiar scenario: Newly returned from a pilgrimage to one of the music's distant hot spots, afire with enthusiasm over the brilliant playing you heard there, you make your way to your local session venue on the usual night, determined to give the listeners a serenading they won't soon forget. But how quickly your mood changes! Within the first ten minutes it becomes clear that something is amiss. Is it the quality of the playing? Possibly. But that's only part of the problem. The rest lies in the nature of the session itself. It's not flowing, it's not breathing, it has no inner logic or natural momentum. It isn't bringing out the best in the musicians, nor is it particularly pleasing the listeners.

This is the moment when you realize that the seeming offhandedness and impromptu grace of a good session are no accident, and that a sense of how to conduct one—and how to conduct yourself *at* one—is not something you're born with after all, your Irish surname notwithstanding. The fact is, these things must be learned, either by example or by outright instruction. And this is no less true for whole towns than for individuals.

If your own town's acquaintance with the music is longstanding and intimate, and examples of upstanding sessioneers are everywhere to be found, then this little book may not be for you. If, however, you happen to be a citizen of one of the Seattles, the Adelaides, the Stuttgarts, the Osakas of this world—in other words, if you live in a place whose local language, flora, fauna, religion, and/or driving, mating, or eating habits distinguish it in no uncertain terms from Ireland—then perhaps an item or two in the following pages will help you get your neighborhood session on track and keep it there. Chances are, it can't make things any worse.

Field Guide to the Irish Music Session is not targeted at musicians alone, however. The question-and-answer format of Part I will provide even the casual listener with a better understanding of sessions' sometimes mysterious inner workings. Each section begins with a question that most anyone happening on an Irish music session—musician, musician's spouse, bartender, holiday reveler, vice squad officer—might reasonably ask. The issue is then addressed as thoroughly and straightforwardly as possible. The Glossary at the end of the book will introduce readers with little prior knowledge of Irish music to some key terms. And for those who consider themselves aficionados, Part II delves a little deeper into some technical matters.

the
nature
of the
session

Did you say <u>session</u>? What's a session?

A session (*seisiún* in Gaelic) is a gathering of Irish traditional musicians for the purpose of celebrating their common interest in the music by playing it together in a relaxed, informal setting, while in the process generally beefing up the mystical cultural mantra that hums along uninterruptedly beneath all manifestations of Irishness worldwide.

C'mon now, what is it really?

A session (*seisiún* in Gaelic) is a gathering of Irish traditional musicians for the purpose of celebrating their common interest in the music by playing it together in a relaxed, informal setting . . . as an elaborate excuse for getting out of the house and spending an evening with friends over a few pints of beer.

Isn't that the same as a "jam"?

Absolutely not. There's no "jamming" in Irish traditional music. Irish music is very specific: specific tunes in specific rhythms, played in specific ways in specific keys on specific instruments. You can't walk into a session unprepared and unschooled and expect to bluff your way through it. You either know how to play this music or you don't; you've either listened to lots of it or you haven't.

More like a concert or a recital, then . . .

Wrong again. Although a few solo performances make for a well-rounded evening, the general aim of a session is to get the maximum number of musicians playing together on the maximum number of tunes.

In the same way, a session is not an occasion for trotting out carefully wrought arrangements, stunts such as following a hornpipe with a reel and then back into another hornpipe, or breaking from a jig into a slipjig (see the Glossary for definitions of all these terms). Those kinds of things fall into the category of *show biz*, fine for entertaining a paying audience from a great height, but unsuited to sessions, which run on different principles altogether.

The session is where the music lives and breathes, where it does its homework, where it flexes its muscles and idly picks its nose. If a musician has a mind to package Irish music for maximum marketability, or polish it to a dazzling sheen, or encase it in amber like some kind of prehistoric gnat, a session is neither the time nor the place to do it.

Then what's the basic operating principle?

It works like this: One musician starts playing a tune, and whoever knows the tune joins in and plays along. The bunch of them play the tune together a few times, and then ... well, what happens next, and why, is discussed later in this book.

Incidentally, the operative word here is *tune* and not *song*. In Irish music, a tune is what you play and a song is what you sing. The only exception is lilting, which is the singing of a tune in odd little nonsense syllables.

how it starts

How does a session get started?

Sessions fall into two basic categories: those that materialize spontaneously, and those that occur regularly at a specific time and place. In the first instance, a musician who happens to cross paths with other musicians may propose that they all sit down and play a little. In Ireland, the standard wording for such a proposal is, "D'ya fancy a few tunes?" The same suggestion, in the United States, might go, "Let's get this over with—I'd like to be home in time for the Bulls game." If everyone present is in the mood, a session results.

In the second category, a bar or club may sponsor an official session one or more times a week. Setting aside a special seating area for the musicians, as well as providing them with free beer, helps to create a hospitable music-making atmosphere.

Because the participants in a spontaneous session have assembled by choice, knowing who their fellow musicians will be— in contrast with a scheduled session, open to all—the odds tend to be in the impromptu session's favor when it comes to musical quality. This is not a sure thing, however; sessions are by nature unpredictable, and a wide range of variables can make for unexpected results.

•

session instruments

What are all these instruments? May I take out my autoharp?

Not just yet. Read this first:

The following instruments are fully welcome and appropriate at any session of traditional Irish music. In other words, you have virtually no grounds for barring the owners of these instruments, no matter how badly they play.

- Fiddle
- Tinwhistle
- Uilleann pipes
- Flute
- Anglo concertina
- Button accordion

(Strangers to some of these instruments can look them up in the Glossary.)

The following instruments are welcome—though not in unlimited quantities—if the persons playing them can do so in a persuasive manner (not that you're in a position to do anything about it if they can't).

- Guitar (maximum one per session)
- Bouzouki (one per session, preferably if there's no guitar, and vice versa)
- Bodhrán (one per session)
- Mandolin (melodies only, no chords)
- Tenor banjo (player must be able to take a joke)

- Piano accordion (not bloody likely, but stranger things have happened)
- Chromatic harmonica
- English concertina
- Piano (absolute maximum of four per session)
- Bones and spoons are occasionally permissible for the sake of quaintness and charm, but the combined number of pairs of either must never exceed one.

It is reasonable to assume that any instrument that's not on either of the previous lists is unwelcome at an Irish session. For the sake of emphasis and clarity, however—that is, to assure that there's no uncertainty over just how unwelcome they are—we list some here. The following have been spotted at one time or another at Irish sessions, and their owners almost surely didn't get the punishment they deserved.

- Percussion instruments such as dumbeks, djembes, bongos, congas, tambourines, and shakers
- Electric bass, stand-up bass, washtub bass, any damn bass at all
- Five-string banjo
- Hammered dulcimer
- Recorder
- Tinwhistles

    in very obscure keys

- Cello, viola
- Amplified guitar
- Didgeridoo
- Clarinet, saxophone

And, since you asked, the autoharp

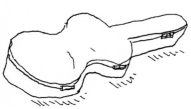

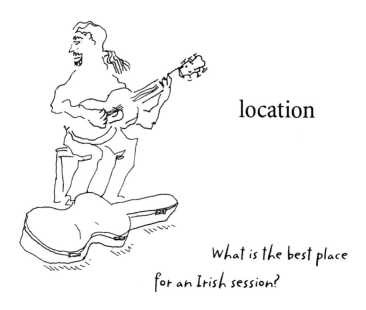

location

What is the best place for an Irish session?

Sessions tend to be at their best when they occur indoors, in close proximity to beer. This can be in a pub/bar, a kitchen, a social club, and so on.

But it's a lovely sunny day—why not play outside?

Theoretically speaking, an outdoor session is feasible if the beer problem can be worked out. However, al fresco sessionizing runs the risk of attracting passersby with guitars who ask, "Hey, do you mind if I *jam* with you guys?" and who are convinced that the accompaniment to "Rakish Paddy" (a famous reel) can't be that awfully different from what you'd play behind, say, "Hoochie Koochie Man" (*not* a famous reel).

A more general problem with outdoor sessions is that, like a fine cheese, Irish musicians tend to be adversely affected by overexposure to fresh air and sunlight. Accustomed as they are to cramped and smoky pubs, they are known to lapse into a morose, disoriented state if dragged to a sandy beach or sylvan glade. Of all the factors that make for high-quality Irish music, it is safe to say that abundant oxygen is near the bottom of the list.

types of tunes

Okay, so what kinds of tunes are played at sessions?

There's an easy answer to this question: reels, reels, and more reels. Jigs come in a distant second, and everything else an even more distant third. An outsize number of non-reels is, for better or worse, a likely sign of a session dominated by beginners, or of one in a locale that is short on links to the living tradition.

On rare occasions, a group of accomplished musicians will treat listeners to a lengthy parade of polkas, barn dances, or some other less common form. This is typically done in a spirit of friendly competition, a "Bet you don't know this one" mentality. When, eventually, those musicians who aren't in the running begin to show their impatience by heaping drink coasters on the table and menacingly setting them afire, the competing players know it's about time to stop. The reels reclaim center stage soon after.

repetitions

How many times do you play each tune?

Musicians differ on how hard to work a given tune before finally moving on to another one. The trend clearly has been toward fewer and fewer repetitions. For proof, listen to recordings from sixty or seventy years ago, when the norm was to repeat a melody so many times that it practically wore a hole in the seat of your pants. Virtually nobody bears down on tunes like that anymore.

Three times through is a common choice nowadays, giving a tune a chance to firmly establish itself without wearing out its welcome. (This applies to two- and three-part tunes played double; those played single often get another repetition or two, whereas especially long ones may be played only twice.) In one locality (is it Philadelphia?), prevailing custom is said to call for four go-rounds. Formal notice regarding the number of repetitions in local use is rare, though ("Welcome to Philadelphia, City of Brotherly Love and Four Iterations of 'The Gander in the Pratie Hole'"), so you may have to ask around.

The tendency to abandon a tune after only two repetitions may reflect the shorter attention spans and lower boredom thresholds that have taken hold since the advent of television. Treating a tune this way, as if it will bruise if handled too much, may provide some cheap thrills, but there is almost an element of hostility to it, as it virtually precludes a musician who doesn't know the tune from getting a handle on it in the short time allotted. A player who attends a particular session regularly shouldn't have to bring a tape recorder to learn tunes. With enough repetitions, they should soak into his brain over the course of time—and two just isn't enough.

And then there are those formidable musicians who won't let go of a tune until they've gnawed every bit of meat off it. That can take time. The experts generally agree that the highest level of Irish musicianship is reached by the player who never plays a tune exactly the same way twice. Recordings of a master such as Bobby Casey of Clare, for example, may exhibit him not so much playing a tune as *living* in it, with epic explorations that require a good few repetitions.

Whatever the consensus on how many run-throughs a tune will get, it is a good idea to make the number clear early on and adhere to it for the duration of the session. Confusion over the matter can lead to irritating false starts and stops. A few unmistakable musical nudges at the outset from one of the stronger players should suffice to set the pattern.

tune
names

Do you have a name for that tune?

Let's see ... "The Humors of Sushi"? No, that's not it ... "My
Love Is in a G-String"? Huh-uh. Darn, I used to know it ...

It's a wonderful thing to know the names of all the tunes one
plays, and there are many gifted musicians who have that knack. For
others, though, it's not so easy. Some reach a point in their musical
careers when, either because their memory capacity is dwindling or
they've found a better use for it, they have to choose between
learning names and learning tunes. Clearly, only a person with a

colossal lack of imagination (or an unhealthy preoccupation with his home computer's alphabetization function) would go for the former.

Anyone who attends sessions regularly will hear many a tune that someone starts up but can't name. Frankly, it's no big deal. Moreover, thanks to a couple of one-size-fits-all titles, no tune need fear finding itself out in the cold. Many otherwise nameless tunes get tagged with the paradoxical Gaelic "*Gan Ainm*," which means "without a name." "The One that Follows It" is a popular title for the tune that everyone knows will come next. Innumerable tunes in the Kerry/Cork style go by "Denis Murphy's" or "O'Keefe's." And finally, you'll get great mileage out of the name "Donohue's" (pronounced Irish-style, not American-style), as in, "I Donohue's tune that one is."

stringing
tunes
together

You've played that one several times—are you going to stop and rest now?

Not yet. Like a cornstalk or a bowling pin, an Irish tune seldom stands alone, and the passage of time in a session is not calibrated in single tunes. Rather, the basic unit of measure is what you might call the Buncha-Tunes-Strung-Together (BTST, for the sake of convenience). The typical BTST is not mapped out ahead of time but comes together naturally tune by tune, and there are tried and true ways of introducing a new tune once the last one has run its course.

Determining who gets to uncork the next tune is simple enough: That privilege falls to the musician who can present the most convincing case for his candidate in the shortest amount of time. His persuasiveness may rely on the fact that he's louder, older, bigger, or more respected, or that he has come up with a more appealing choice than anyone else. Or it may be that he just happened to beat the rest to the punch.

Once a tune has been played as many times as local custom or the mood of the gathering mandates, and the playing has come around to the last part of the tune's last go-round, it's time to spring into action and set up the next one. This happens in one of the following ways:

1. Sometimes tradition, local or general, dictates that a specific tune is the appropriate partner to the one you're playing.

"The Woman of the House," for instance, is a frequent follow-up to "The Morning Dew"; Michael Coleman's "Tarbolton"/"The Longford Collector"/"The Sailor's Bonnet" is another classic combination. A simple nod exchanged between players is a way of saying, "Let's do the one that follows it."

2. Sometimes a musician will shout out the name of the next tune as the previous one is ending. Given the fulfillment of a couple of conditions, first that he can actually be heard doing so (not always the case), and second that his choice is one the other players can live with—which they'll usually indicate by offering up no reaction whatsoever—then that is the tune that will be played. Occasionally another player will object to the item on offer, in which case he'll shout out an alternative. In such cases the second choice virtually always wins out, if only because there isn't time to argue about it. Nonetheless, to keep things friendly, a good musician won't make a habit of second-guessing his session mates this way.

3. In a third approach, when a tune winds to a close, one player simply starts up a new one, without calling out any name at all. Because, obviously, nothing's preventing several people from doing this at the same time, the situation can give rise to a moment of exquisite tension whose resolution rests on the complex interaction of primal instincts understood only by anthropologists. The victor is often the group's alpha male or alpha female (see Glossary), if there is one and if he or she chooses to assume that role.

Regardless of whose tune gets played, this is absolutely not the time for a musician to hold out for his favorite and stubbornly play on against the current. One should learn to spot a winner quickly and then bow out gracefully. There'll be more opportunities later on.

Another option deserves mention here, namely the rather uncommon practice of specifying in advance what tunes will be played and in what order. Though perhaps useful in educational settings, this approach has two fundamental weaknesses. First, such precise, thorough planning somehow seems out of place in the kind of establishment where a typical customer might be expected to put the finishing touch on a convivial evening by vomiting all over his shoes. Second, it precludes the possibility of a surprising, delightfully inspired choice of tunes arrived at on the spur of the moment.

But how do you know which tune
is the right one to play next?

The tune a musician chooses to play next may have that honor for the simple reason that it is the only one she can think of at the time. If, on the other hand, several come to mind and she wants to pick just the right one, she should remember that part of the fun of the well-crafted BTST is the generation of a little thrill, a little rush of release, at the start of each new tune.

The surest way to achieve this is to change keys. If not a key change, then a change of modes is recommended, as in minor to major. If the next tune is going to be in the same key, it should at least be different in feel from the last: There may be a certain poetic symmetry to playing a whole chain of gloomy-sounding E-minor reels, but in practice it can be boring.

A crucial thing to watch for in tune changes is that the tempo and rhythm are maintained. Missed or extra beats or a clumsy pause have a way of punching a big, ugly hole in what would otherwise have been a dramatic transition. Mastering the smooth changeover can be a challenge to beginning musicians, but it is an indispensable skill.

how boring irish music is

Despite what you say about the differences between tunes, they all sound alike to me. Is there something wrong with my ears?

Not at all. Of course all Irish music sounds alike. That's how you tell it's Irish music. That's how you know you haven't walked in on a session of Macedonian or Senegalese music by mistake. That's how you know that when you walk into a music store and ask for Irish music, you won't be sold something that sounds like Miles Davis or the Kinks. Pretty handy, if you think about it.

tuning

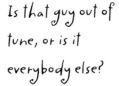

Is that guy out of tune, or is it everybody else?

Although it meant a little less to previous generations, today there is general agreement that playing in tune is a good thing. Pauses between tunes are an excellent time to check whether one's tuning drifted during the last medley.

Some instruments are universally tunable, others somewhat tunable, and others not tunable at all. It makes obvious sense for the group to tune to that instrument whose pitch can't be changed, such as a piano, concertina, accordion, harmonica, or untunable tinwhistle. If more than one of those are present, you can only hope they're in tune with each other. If not, then any player whose instrument can't reach the generally attainable pitch must do the honorable thing and drop out.

Uilleann pipes are tunable within a certain narrow range. In the absence of any of the instruments named above, let the piper set the pitch, and then cross your fingers that he'll be able to maintain it. Frequent revisiting of his "A" is advisable.

As for the increasingly common electronic tuner, first of all, it won't do you much good if one of the group's instruments can't reach concert pitch. Second, there's something weirdly intrusive and irrelevant about the presence of these gadgets at a session—not much different or less nerdy, really, than bringing a cellular phone. Why not leave it at home?

tempo

How fast should the tunes be played?

Apprentice Irish musicians often have earnest, moralistic discussions about the tempo at which tunes should be played. And yet, players who are more seasoned talk about it less. Why is that?

As painful as it is to admit, a musician tends to think the music's being played too fast when he himself has trouble keeping up with it. Once his skills improve and he's able to handle a quicker tempo, he notices it—and complains about it—less.

This is not to say that an individual won't have preferences. When playing solo, every musician naturally reverts to the tempo that works best for him. The comfort level can vary by instrument: It's easier to play fast than slow on a whistle or flute, for instance, whereas with a fiddle or pipes the opposite can be true. Tunes, too, sometimes incline one way or the other: A simple tune like "The Sligo Maid" wants to be played at a pretty lively clip, while some of the convoluted (albeit beautiful) reels composed by Ed Reavy barely want to be played at all.

Good sessions come in a wide variety of speeds. The reels at the wonderful sessions led by John Kelly and sons at Dublin's Four Seasons pub in the late 1970s, for example, were played at a relaxed, almost stately pace, yet those at many another gathering can fly by fast enough to blow the nearby ashtrays clean. A fast tempo is no more a guarantee of good music than a slow one.

A case could be made that when it comes to giving the music the right feel (and opinions vary greatly as to what the right feel is), it takes a pretty able player to put good rhythm and "lift" into slow music, whereas high-speed playing is more effective at masking outright sloppiness. It might be more agreeable to the ear, then, for mediocre musicians to race through a tune and get it over with.

When all is said and done, an Irish musician needs to be versatile. Don't forget that this is meant to be dance music, and although you may coast along for years playing at a leisurely, low-pressure pace in your own

living room, there's bound to come a point when a group of dancers asks you to accompany them at breakneck speed. Doing so will mean sacrificing all claims to musicality or coherence—the only remaining distinguishing feature of your playing will be the beat. But dancers aren't often accused of knowing a lot about music, and they probably won't notice a thing.

When it comes to session playing, the better musicians are able to accommodate most anyone's tempo and will do so in the interest of giving the music as clear and homogeneous a sound as possible. That kind of uniformity is what makes a session enjoyable to play and listen to. Many a session outside Ireland falls on its face because no two participants arrive with the same approach to rhythm and tempo, and too many of them are either unwilling or unable to find common musical ground. Each player who starts a tune does so with a different feel and speed, and the end product is a fickle mishmash that makes listeners wonder why this seemingly antagonistic group bothered to come together in the first place. Moreover, the strain of shifting gears every ten minutes can take a lot of the fun out of playing. A good session is a confident session, and one that can't settle on a common tempo after a little while sounds anything but confident.

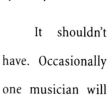

But that last tune started off slow and then sped up . . .

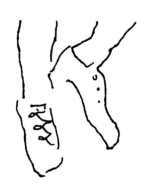

It shouldn't have. Occasionally one musician will editorialize on another's choice of tempos by forcing the music up to a speed that he prefers (oddly enough, virtually no one ever slows a tune down). The result is music that is unsure of itself and hard to follow. The only safeguard against this is good manners, and it's good manners—as well as good taste—to finish a tune at the tempo at which it began, whether it suits you or not.

dynamics

Why is the music all the same volume?

Irish music's most traditional instruments aren't known for their huge dynamic ranges. Whistle, wooden flute, pipes—these might as well have an ON/OFF switch for all the difference in volume they can muster. As for the violin, folkloric fiddling styles seldom allow for the *piano*-to-*forte* capabilities of classical technique.

One of the principal offenders in the volume department used to be the ubiquitous Paolo Soprani accordion. Happily, those are rapidly being replaced by quieter models, a development that's heartening to everyone but accordionists. Banjos, similarly, tend to be as loud as they're made to be rather than as they're played to be. A brassy-sounding banjo stays brassy no matter how soft the picker's stroke. A few minor adjustments can tone down the instrument's brashness if desired, but so far no banjo player has ever desired it. Hence all the banjo jokes.

The lesson embedded in all this is that an instrument's possession of a wide dynamic range is God's way of telling its player to gravitate toward the quiet end of the spectrum at sessions. This applies most decidedly to accompaniment instruments: piano, guitar, bodhrán, bouzouki.

accompaniment

But there's got to be accompaniment, right?

By no means. Irish music was in fine shape before it began to be swaddled in lush, melodramatic harmonies, and it would be in equally fine shape if all chord-playing instruments (including accordionists' left hands) were to disappear tomorrow. Irish dance tunes were designed to stand on their own, without accompaniment, and they still do so quite admirably. In the final analysis, every accompanist must acknowledge a cruel but indisputable truth, which is that what she is doing is, let's face it, superfluous to the music. Not that guitarists should let this news get them down—it's too late to turn the clock back now. They should, however, let it inspire a little humility and discretion.

pauses

Hey, why did it get so quiet all of a sudden?

Even the most brilliant BTST must eventually come to an end, and when it does, it's time for a little rest. A good session necessarily includes pauses, some of which may be quite long. A pause between bouts of playing is a sign of ease and confidence on the musicians' part. It's their opportunity to catch their breath, have a drink of beer, light up a cigarette (unless they live on the West Coast of the United States, of course), chat with the person next door, tune up, suggest that someone else tune up, and generally act as if they have a life worth living.

A musician who can't help pouncing on the first particle of dead time to start a tune—even if that silence was preceded by twenty uninterrupted minutes of music—can seem pathetic and overeager. He also may be advertising the fact that he doesn't have many tunes and is desperate to start up the handful he has, lest no one else do it for him in the course of the evening. This is not a flattering impression to give a roomful of strangers.

To think of sessions as strictly musical events is to harbor a misunderstanding. They are also social events. The musician who pours his whole heart into the playing but ignores the social give-and-take is not only a bore to play with, he also doesn't do the music any favors. Nothing takes the starch out of a session like someone who's so infatuated with the music itself that he can't look the other players in the eye.

playing and listening

The session's only half over— why are those musicians leaving?

Somewhere in a movie or novel, a character once spoke a memorable line something like, "I'm polite to people, Johnny, for the very same reason you're *not*—'cause that's the way we were brought up."

A similar case of identical causes but contrasting effects applies to sessions, in the sense that a person who plays Irish music attends for the very same reason as a person who only listens. The reason is that he or she likes to hear Irish music. A good musician isn't likely to be there to hear himself—he can do that just fine at home, where the beer's cheaper and he doesn't risk running into any ex-girlfriends. On the contrary, a musician attends a session in hopes of hearing as good a spell of Irish music as possible. He goes to hear it, and if in the course of doing that he happens to end up playing some too, well, that's just grand. But it's not the most important thing.

Some less-than-accomplished musicians have a hard time grasping this concept. They apparently attend sessions in order to hear themselves (and, by logical implication, to let other lucky souls hear them). Because they are, as far as they're concerned, the star attraction, they are often seen packing up and heading home once they've exhausted their store of tunes, or once it looks as if the other musicians don't plan to sample from that same store.

The truth is, they couldn't pick a worse time to leave. Instead of sticking around, soaking up the music and the atmosphere in general, learning new tunes that will enhance their participation in future sessions, studying the better players' technique, and getting a couple more free beers, these players make tracks. They leave precisely when they should be settling in for a good long listen.

This music is above all an aural/oral tradition, and that will remain true no matter how many collections of Irish music are ever published. The only path to playing this stuff is listening to it. Without listening, there's nothing to practice. In Irish music, listening *is* practice.

repertoire

All right, I'm hooked.
What tunes should I learn first?

Every one you can get your hands on. And not only reels, either, despite what's been said about their constituting the bulk of a session—you never know when a mazurka or fling might spring out from some well-concealed hiding place. A serious Irish musician lives in a state of permanent low-level anxiety over how many tunes she doesn't yet know.

It's common among beginning players of Irish music to resolve to learn only those tunes that really appeal to them. This makes them feel tasteful and discerning. But a little experience soon proves such a campaign to be a waste of time.

Sure, there will always be favorite and less favored tunes. But at the end of the day it comes down to this: The more tunes you know, the more playing you'll get to do. So learn 'em all, anywhere you can. Go to the same session over and over until you've picked up all the local hits. Listen. Learn from commercial recordings, archival recordings, books (that is, if you know how to flesh out the bare bones of musical notation to make it sound like Irish music). Listen. Learn them over the phone, in your car, off the radio. Learn from real live people as much as possible. Listen. Learn twenty tunes that everyone knows and then one that nobody knows—this will make you both an interesting player and a valuable source of tunes. LISTEN.

It may be instructive here, in a negative way, to mention an Irish tradition called the "party piece." A party piece is a little turn that a person performs when called on to provide homegrown entertainment at a social gathering. For one person it will be the recitation of a poem, for another the singing of a song, for another a little dance step; another will play a tune on the tinwhistle.

As with karaoke, the performance of a party piece is seldom expected to be good but rather merely endearing or even impressive in its own modest way. Above all, it's familiar: Uncle Donal has been reciting that same poem at parties for forty-five years now, and he'll be doing it till the day he dies.

What does the notion of a party piece have to do with sessions? Simply this: If your repertoire is so small that your regular session mates can count on you to haul out your own party piece, that very same old worn-out tune time after time and week after week, unvarying, as if you carried the poor thing around with you everywhere in a velvet-lined box—well then, you've got too few tunes, and you'd better get to work. Do the world a favor and learn some new ones.

when and what *not* to play

I don't know the tune you're playing—may I strum along anyway?

Not if you know what's good for you. Take note of the following: *The fact that you are holding a musical instrument in your hands at a session does not automatically entitle you to play it.*

As stated elsewhere in this book, Irish music is a very specific thing—specific tunes played on specific instruments in specific ways. Your right to participate in a session hinges on your understanding of what the music is about, where it came from, and where your particular instrument fits into it, if indeed it does at all. Even in America, Land of the Free, your mere presence at a session does not grant you the right to join in.

Given that your instrument is acceptable at an Irish session in the first place (see the section on instruments), there are still certain things you may not do. Foremost among them is noodling. Noodling is the endless, pointless probing and exploring of a melody by someone who doesn't know it, the playing of little snippets and phrases that (if you're lucky) may follow the general contour of the tune but in fact aren't the tune itself. Noodling is very irritating and distracting to other players and skews the overall sound.

Irish music is a unisonal, not polyphonic, art form. Apart from occasionally dropping down an octave, à la some Kerry/Cork fiddlers, the idea is for all the melodic instruments to play the same notes at the same time. If you're clueless about a tune, refrain from improvising lovely little harmonizing lines to go along with it. They don't belong.

It's no less offensive for an accompaniment instrument to noodle, as the player searches here and there, often at great length, for the right chords to go with a tune he's never heard. Guitarists who play in DADGAD tuning, in particular, seem to abhor a vacuum and want to hammer away whether they know where the music's going or not. Their tuning's orientation toward octaves and fifths probably makes them think they can get away with it.

The anti-noodling rule doesn't mean that someone who has nearly memorized a tune, or who is quick at picking tunes up, can't quietly, discreetly work her way through it. That is a legitimate part of the learning process. But as an end in itself, idle plucking, strumming, or tootling is a very unwelcome intrusion.

tin whistle

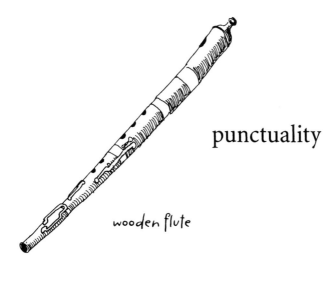

wooden flute

punctuality

The paper said the session would start at nine o'clock. It's ten already, and no one's playing—did I come on the wrong night?

Probably not. Unfortunately for the punctilious among us, there is no such thing as punctuality when it comes to a session. Each one has a unique, unpredictable rhythm of its own, and there's no telling when the good stuff might begin or end. The best music can take place in the first half-hour, the last, or anyplace in between.

Later is more likely, though, so if you come early plan to stay late, and if you come late plan to play really well.

One thing for a musician to keep in mind is that arriving late increases the chances that the others will already have played your favorite tunes. If you should sit down and start one up and be greeted by nothing but snickers or stony silence, you'll know why. Your companions may join in just to humor you, but they're under no obligation to do so.

encouragement

Why are you all so nice to each other?

A session and a concert are two very different things, and a key difference between them is the level of background noise. In stark contrast to the courteous quietude of a concert hall, an Irish session is expected to rise like a cluster of methane bubbles out of a sea of talk, laughter, clinking glasses, and skidding cash-register drawers, and to make its own contribution to the general clamor in turn.

Not all of the ambient chatter comes from the bar's patrons. The musicians themselves traditionally supply a portion of it, with shouted comments of encouragement, admiration, exultation, or vilification. To the untrained ear, what motivates such remarks can be a little hard to figure out. A player who launches into a bit of genuinely impressive solo work may be urged on by shouts of "Lovely!" or "Good man!" or "Good girl!" (no letters, please, about the implied sexist bias). Someone who knows where the musician comes from might boost his birthplace, as in "Up Kerry!"

On the other hand, a poor performance may be greeted by the very same praise. This paradoxical behavior can reflect: (1) the belief that with enough encouragement and hard work this particular musician actually will improve; (2) an interest in maintaining the session's chummy air despite stern disapproval of the way the tune's being butchered; or (3) a desire to stay on the player's good side because, despite his/her second-rate musicianship, you still find him/her very sexy and attractive and are hoping for a chance to slip your hand down his/her Levi's before the night is through.

discouragement

Why are you all so mean to each other?

The opposite of praising is "slagging," the Irish term for heaping gratuitous criticism or abuse on someone just for the fun of seeing him squirm. An expert slagger knows how to precipitate a string of uncomfortable little jolts of insecurity in the victim while forcing him to wear a smile all the while—obviously a very delicate and sophisticated art. Solo slagging is not unheard of, but the technique is at its ripest and most artistic when perpetrators attack en masse.

For an example of slagging, let's return to our original soloist, a fiddler who is tripping his way through an astonishingly handsome rendition of "Jenny's Welcome to Charley." The reaction he gets is not necessarily what you'd expect, considering the work he's doing. While a few earnest shouts of "Lovely!" come from people who don't know him personally, his closest friends voice very different sentiments. "Bollocks!" cries one. "Play one you know!" shouts another. A third pleads, "Practice at home!"

A charming and affectionate race, the Irish.

singing

Is anybody going to sing?

The ideal session is punctuated at intervals by offerings from a singer or two. Some rare sessions even regularly alternate tunes with songs—though that would seem to call for an unnatural degree of organization. The inclusion of singing, especially unaccompanied singing, rounds out an evening of traditional music in a heartwarming way. Occasionally one of the instrumentalists is good for a song, and of course guitar players may sing as well.

Singers are sometimes bashful about injecting a voice into a situation dominated by instruments (the more bashful they are, the better singers they tend to be), so the players should be alert to the presence of a singer in their midst and be prepared to call for a song at various points in the session. Once a song is called for, it helps the vocalist if you try and quiet the surrounding crowd a little. This can be difficult or even dangerous, depending on the neighborhood, but it's worth a try if you can get away with it. At the very least, the musicians should pay the singer the courtesy of keeping their own mouths shut, so the voice can be heard clearly in the immediate area even if not throughout the premises. Finally, it's customary to compliment the singer when she's finished, or even while she's singing, and that applies whether she's any good or not.

facing facts

Well, Doctor, I've tried my level best, and I'm still a bad musician. Does that mean I'm a bad person?

Not necessarily. It does oblige you, however, to acknowledge and accept the fact that there are better musicians than you.

Statistics dictate that the typical session will be made up of some better players and some worse ones. True, nature occasionally creates mutations: In the course of your playing career you're bound to run across a few sessions (more than a few and you should consider moving to another city) populated solely by bad musicians. By the same token, at some point you'll be lucky enough to happen on one of those legendary gatherings in which every player is an expert—so much so that inserting yourself into the lineup would lower the tone of the event to an unacceptable degree (so don't).

Those freaks of nature aside, it's safe to assume that most of your playing will be done with a mix of the accomplished and the less so. No matter how thin-skinned you are (and you may have guessed by now that this is not a music for the thin-skinned), be assured that the better players aren't there to shame you, snub you, embarrass you, or otherwise assert their superiority in obnoxious ways. For the most part, they have better things to do. They, like you, are simply out for a tune and a pint. The fact that they know tunes you don't, and that they play "your" tunes better than you can, is not grounds for bathing them in delicate little ripples of silent resentment or jealousy. Nor is it an excuse for throwing up your hands in desperation and slinking home. They're better than you, and that's all there is to it. Accept that fact and appreciate them for it.

Yes, appreciate these musicians, if not as people—and some will make that difficult—then as transmitters of the tradition. Appreciate them as the sources of tunes and technique that they are, and that you can't do without. Appreciate the fact that by merely lifting their hung-over little heads off the pillow in the morning, they contribute to sustaining Irish music, a tradition without which you'd be missing out on a lot of good times. There is much to learn from them—don't squander the opportunity.

Not that superior talent or greater experience is a license to pull rank and act like a jerk. A measure of graciousness is expected of stronger musicians as well as weaker ones. Although it's the hotshots' job to make the music as convincing and exciting as possible, they ought not ruthlessly monopolize the session or deliberately put less adept players into a suicidal frame of mind. It's standard practice, for instance, for the ace to compliment and encourage the novices, just as they will sometimes compliment him.

You will save yourself considerable grief if you avoid saddling Irish music sessions with expectations they can't possibly fulfill and were never meant to. One such vain hope is that a session will serve as a model of democracy in action (not surprisingly, subscribers to this misconception tend to be American). While democracy has undeniable merits as a system of governance, its relevance to Irish music-making is nearly nil. When the objective is to play and hear the best music possible, it stands to reason that there might come a point in the evening when you must step aside and let the best musicians do just that.

Nor should you expect playing in a session to give you the opportunity—finally!—to express the deepest stirrings of your tormented, sensitive soul. Not that this can't happen—on occasion it does. But holding the session and your fellow musicians hostage to this very private, personal longing is unrealistic and unfair. Practically speaking, they have other business to attend to, namely providing entertainment and a pleasant, civil way to pass the time.

the importance of sessions

When all is said and done, isn't it simpler to go to a concert or buy a recording?

Maybe. There's only one problem, which is that without sessions there'd *be* no concerts or recordings.

The session is the wellspring of Irish music, its beating heart. Its importance to the tradition must never be forgotten. The sometimes tricky, overrehearsed material that finds its way onto recordings and the stage may maintain a higher profile, but it owes its vitality to the decades of sessions that preceded it and gave shape to the music. What is all that fancy stuff, anyway, but the self-conscious stepchild of the classic session in a pub or friendly kitchen? And what is all its cleverness but an attempt to reproduce the verve and heart of a good session?

True, there are bad sessions and good ones, and in terms of ratios the former well outnumber the latter. This world being the yin-yang sort of place it is, each kind of session surely has its purpose—although it's hard to imagine what a consistently bad session can accomplish that mild food poisoning or a bee between your toes couldn't do quicker.

The specter of Bad Music is only too ready to rear its ugly head at all times in the hinterlands of Irish music, and session players must be ever vigilant. What can turn a session bad? The list is long: musicians who can't keep a beat; instruments or intonation that are grossly out of tune; too many guitars, too many bodhráns, too many bouzoukis; deafening accordions with galumphing left hands; obnoxious percussionists who mistakenly wander in on their way to a neo-pagan drumming circle; musicians who slavishly imitate their favorite recordings, even down to the mistakes; musicians who can't be bothered to learn new tunes; musicians too drunk to play but too inconsiderate to pass out; too many uncommon tunes; too many common tunes; terrible acoustics; not enough laughs; "Last call!"; musicians who don't listen to one another or don't allow others to get a word in edgewise. In sum, considering how many things can go wrong, it's a wonder the music is ever good.

And yet it is. At times it's very good indeed. A session that's really humming along, with an unstoppable momentum born of a combination of good musicianship, good intentions, and good humor, a session that gives full play to the riotousness, sweetness, sturdiness, sadness, and exultation that blend so uniquely in traditional Irish music, is about as exciting and rewarding an experience as one can have without needing to get up and draw the curtains.

But a good session is not a free-for-all. There's more discipline to it than its apparent casualness and spontaneity would suggest. That discipline arises naturally, unforced, out of the musicians' respect for the music and their thorough familiarity with it. Both elements are essential: Respect without familiarity is a recipe for bad music, while familiarity without respect is a recipe for bad temper. Accord the tradition the respect it deserves, and do your homework, and Irish music will reward you amply and often for many years to come.

Which is not to say you should quit your day job.

Is there anything else I should know about Irish sessions?

Yes: Tip the bartender.

answers to some
often-asked
questions
about
the origins
of the
Irish
traditional
music
session

When did sessions originate?

Scholars have yet to determine this with any degree of accuracy.

Where was the first session held?

The historical evidence is insufficient to provide a conclusive answer to this question.

What instruments were involved in the earliest sessions?

It's difficult to tell.

Did the first session musicians play seated or standing up?

The jury is still out on that one, we're afraid.

Do historians have any idea which tunes were played in early sessions?

Funny you should ask.

Was there a particular region of Ireland where sessions first took root?

Check back with us on this.

Did the earliest sessions consist entirely of men, or did women play also?

That's a puzzler!

some of the finer points

Is there any one feature that has traditionally distinguished the Irish session from gatherings of musicians from other cultures?

Yes.

do-it-yourself
tune names based
on
established
favorites from
*O'Neill's Music of
Ireland*
(published 1903)

**TITLES IN WHICH TO INSERT THE
NAME OF A PLACE:**

"The Humors of _____"

"The _____ Lasses"

"The _____ Races"

"The Boys of _____"

"The Rakes of _____"

TITLES IN WHICH TO INSERT THE NAME OF
A BODY OF WATER:

"The Banks of _____"

TITLES IN WHICH TO INSERT THE NAME OF A PERSON:

"_____'s Fancy"

"_____'s Favorite"

"Young _____"

TITLES IN WHICH TO INSERT THE NAME OF A RICH PERSON WHO INHABITED A LARGE, LOVELY HOUSE DURING THE HEYDAY OF THE ITINERANT IRISH HARPERS:

"Planxty _____"

TITLES IN WHICH TO INSERT A SURNAME ONLY:

"Miss _____"

some of the finer points

TITLES IN WHICH TO INSERT THE NAME OF
AN ITEM OF NAUTICAL CLOTHING:

"The Sailor's _____"

TITLES IN WHICH TO INSERT THE NAME OF A TYPE OF FRUIT:

"The _____ Blossom"

TITLES IN WHICH TO INSERT THE NAME OF A TYPE OF TREE:

"The _____ Tree"

TITLES IN WHICH TO INSERT THE NAME OF MOST ANYTHING, ANYPLACE, OR ANYONE AT ALL:

"The Yellow _____"

"Farewell to _____"

"The Green _____"

"Jackson's _____"

"The Jolly _____"

"The Maid of/on/in/behind the _____"

"The Merry _____"

"The New _____"

"The Old _____"

the hornpipe
question

A jig is a jig, for the most part, and its 6/8 time is not open to much interpretation. Not so with reels, which can exhibit huge rhythmic differences from one player to the next. Until not too long ago, regional styles exercised considerable influence over players' rhythms, and a quick listen to someone's reels furnished information enough for an educated guess as to where she came from.

This is no longer true. With the huge increase in the recording and marketing of Irish music, as well as more frequent and extensive travel by musicians, regional styles are nearly a thing of the past. Arising in their place are personal styles, usually amalgams of several ways of playing with any number of peculiar idiosyncrasies thrown in.

Regardless of individual variations in approach, there's a healthy natural tendency for all musicians at a session to fall into line when it comes to reel playing. Indeed, one mark of a good Irish musician is his ability to conform his playing to others' when necessary, and his willingness to do so. The conditions that determine which rhythm prevails are pretty much the same as those that determine tempo (see "Alpha Male/Female" in the Glossary).

So much for reels. Hornpipes are something else again. There are two basic rhythms for hornpipes, with only minimal variation in between. The first, bouncier and generally favored by fiddles and accordions, consists of what are called dotted rhythms (though they are never notated in dotted rhythms in books). This rhythm goes something like DAH da-DAH da-DAH da-DAH, da-DAH da-DAH da-DAH.

The second is squarer, less frilly, more driving. Often played by flutes, and the clear favorite of many pipers, it goes DA-DA-DA-DA-DA-DA-DA-DA-DA-DA-DA-DA-DA.

The funny thing is, whereas divergent reel rhythms usually find a common groove in which to coexist, the two contrasting hornpipe styles are almost impossible to meld. Playing next to someone who's in the opposing hornpipe camp is a lot like being poked with a butter knife at a metronome speed of, oh, 110 for three minutes straight. Hardly lethal, but not exactly unadulterated pleasure either.

And what is the solution? To be honest, there isn't one—you just do the best you can and hope no one notices. The only reason the author has brought up the matter here is to impress you with his analysis of the situation. Thanks for your interest.

the question
of key

Picture this scenario:

An Irish session. A cold February night. In between tunes, you're discussing the pros and cons of the global economy with the musician sitting on your left. Suddenly, in midsentence, your ears prick up at the sound of the first few bars of a reel coming from the fiddler across the way.

But this is not just any old reel. This is a reel you learned only a couple of days ago, and you're very proud of your mastery of it.

Doing your best not to appear rude, you break off the conversation and hoist up your trustworthy antique flute to join in. To your shock and dismay, however, your joint effort produces nothing like beautiful music. Instead of a mellifluous blending, the duet sounds like cockatiel karaoke. Brokenhearted, you give up.

What has gone wrong? The answer is simple: The fiddler is playing in the wrong key. Your problem is, it's nearly impossible for you to play in the wrong key with him.

But why should the fiddler shoulder all the blame—couldn't it be *you* who's in the wrong? Possible, but not likely. This is because the mechanics of whistles, pipes, and wooden flutes severely limit the number of keys they can comfortably play in. Because most traditional Irish tunes were conceived precisely for those instruments, the chances are good that any key other than the original one will be hard to manage. Fiddles are a different story. A fiddle, as everyone knows, has both black and white keys—far more flexible in this department.

Hijacking a tune into a novel key used to be a rare and exotic exercise. Playing "The Star of Munster" in G-minor instead of

A-minor was a racy thing to do twenty years ago. Not so anymore.
Irish music is now cheaper and easier to record than ever before, and market pressures plus the influence of other musics now drive traditional musicians to innovate, innovate, innovate. Bumping tunes up or down into new keys is one way of doing that.

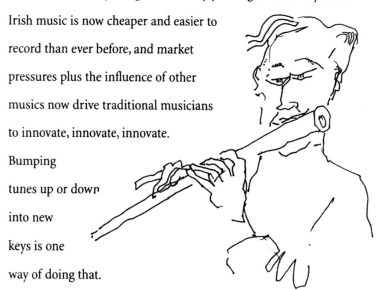

The trouble is, once a recording achieves a certain degree of popularity, its contents have a way of becoming gospel, especially among newer players and more especially in far-flung locales that rely heavily on recordings of Irish music rather than the real, in-person thing. Enthusiastic fiddlers rush to learn the tune in the new key, not even realizing that it *is* a new key and that before the album's release no one but that particular band played it that way. Flutists and pipers, meanwhile, are left scratching their heads, wondering where they'll find the money to buy an instrument in the key of C.

As stated elsewhere in this book, a recording and a session are very different things, and what adds color and marketability to one may be pure sabotage to the other. Rampant key-tampering hardly seems the best way to foster a mutually satisfying, cooperative Irish session scene. Even in this day and age, there are some activities that ought to be confined to the privacy of one's own home . . . or a recording studio.

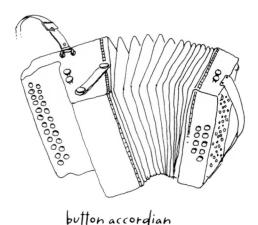

button accordian

GLOSSARY

Accompaniment: The playing of chords on one instrument to go along with the playing of a melody on another. A recent antitrust suit in the California Supreme Court charged a cartel of guitar and bouzouki manufacturers with promoting the notion that accompaniment is appropriate for Irish traditional music at all times. The case is still pending.

Accordion (also called the "box"): Except in a scant few cases, Irish traditional accordionists play the version of this instrument that substitutes two rows of buttons for a piano-style keyboard. Formerly the loudest weapon in the Irish arsenal, button accordions are now made in sweeter-sounding styles—which, sad to say, makes banjos seem all the louder.

Alpha Male/Female: A scientific term, applied to Irish music in this book for the very first time (gosh, I wonder why). Refers to the most feared or respected individual in a

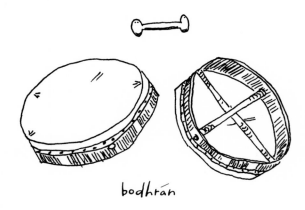

bodhrán

group affiliated by kinship or some other bond. Musically speaking, the woman with the loudest instrument, or the man with the biggest one.

Banjo: Apart from the fact that it has four strings instead of five, it's tuned entirely differently, it lacks a drone note, its neck is shorter, it's played with a single flat pick rather than finger picks, and its players seldom wear string ties, the banjo played in Irish music is identical to the one used in American bluegrass.

Bodhrán (pronounced "bow-ron"): Ireland's contribution to the world of percussion. A large, single-headed hand drum that no one wants to hear but everyone wants to play.

Bouzouki: Originally a long-necked Greek stringed instrument with a potato-bug body, the bouzouki emigrated to Ireland some time ago (just when everyone else was leaving!), underwent a few design modifications, and set up shop as an accompaniment instrument that's a little lighter on its feet than a guitar. There hasn't been a peep from the Greek embassy.

BTST: Short for "Buncha-Tunes-Strung-Together," a term coined by James Joyce, who used it repeatedly (with a somewhat different spelling) in early drafts of *Finnegans Wake*. Later, on his editor's advice, the writer all but abandoned the expression; it appears only once in the 1939 edition, on page 411, where it is formed vertically by the first letters of lines 6 through 34.

Concertina: A squeezebox favored by the musicians of County Clare, the concertina comes in two types. "English" concertinas produce the same note on one button whether the hands are pushing together or drawing apart. "Anglo" (short for "Anglo-German") models sound a different note on the push than on the draw, a trait that adds rhythmic liveliness and makes Anglo concertinas the hands-down favorite of Irish players.

DADGAD (pronounced "dadgad"): A method of tuning a guitar so that strumming the open strings produces the notes named. The invention of DADGAD, now so popular among Irish accompanists, marked a revolutionary advancement

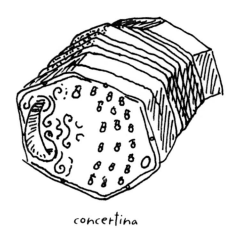

concertina

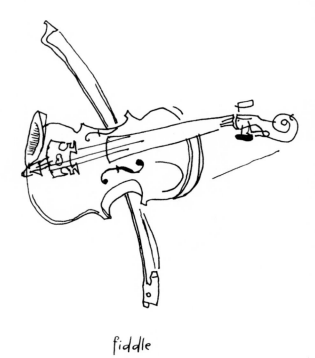

fiddle

over primitive standard tuning, which required that guitarists actually listen to the people they were accompanying.

Fiddle: Identical to a violin, except when it's played by a violinist, in which case it *is* a violin.

Flute: The standard Irish flute is made of wood, not metal, and has open holes rather than keys. Compared with the modern silver flute it is very primitive, and yet it remains the instrument of choice for most Irish flutists, not to mention flautists.

Harmonica: Playing Irish music on the harmonica is an exhausting and almost certainly unhygienic pursuit, and yet a handful of hardy souls continue to demonstrate that it can be done well. They do it not on little palm-sized diatonic (the equivalent of only the white keys on the piano) harps like the ones Bob Dylan and Mick Jagger play, but on larger, heftier chromatic (both black and white keys) models that are ridiculously costly and in constant need of repair.

Hornpipe: Not, as some people seem to think, an instrument, but a kind of Irish tune in 4/4 time. Think of Popeye's theme, but a little slower—no, not "I'm Popeye the sailor man, etc.," which is in waltz time, but the perky little number that's heard whenever the spinach begins to take effect. And a little slower.

Jig: A tune in 6/8 time, the kind everyone automatically associates with Irish music. "The Irish Washerwoman" is an example.

Lilting: "Dum-diddly-diddly-dum, di-de-leedl-di, deedl-leedl-deedl-dum, di-de-leedl dum"—which is harder than it looks.

Noodling: The bane of any Irish session, noodling is a kind of reflex action performed by someone who has brought an instrument but is embarrassed to be seen not playing it. The aural equivalent of twiddling the thumbs or chewing the fingernails, at times it produces a sound eerily similar to the music from *Riverdance.*

Party Piece: A favorite song, tune, or recitation performed for a mostly sympathetic audience at a social gathering. A ready source of cheap, non-union entertainment for centuries, the party-piece tradition ultimately succumbed to the onslaught of television. In fact, the beginnings of its demise have been precisely traced to a night in April 1965 when a Mr. Conor Driscoll of Ferbane, County Offaly, instead of his usual stirring rendition of "Four Green Fields," regaled a house full of guests with the theme song from *Bonanza*.

Pint: A measure of time equal to fifteen reels, three jigs, and a hornpipe in the United States, and approximately half that in Ireland and the countries of the British Commonwealth.

Polka: A type of quick, jaunty tune in 2/4 time that is regarded with much affection in the southwest corner of Ireland and generally scorned or ignored elsewhere.

Polyphony: According to *The American Heritage Dictionary,* "music with two or more independent melodic parts sounded together." Being considerably more interesting than normal Irish music, polyphony is obviously unacceptable at sessions.

Reel: The Irish musician's favorite type of tune—the fast one (unless played slowly).

Slagging: If you don't know already, we're not telling you—you clueless, bog-trotting *amadán*. Have a nice day.

Slipjig: A tune in 9/8 time whose chief distinguishing characteristic is the difficulty of telling where it begins and ends.

Tinwhistle: A rudimentary metal or plastic tube with six holes in it, which makes a high-pitched, tootley sound. Requiring prissy, delicate breathing and insectlike finger movements, it's not exactly an instrument you can sink your teeth into; still, in the right hands it makes excellent music, and at a bargain price. Also called pennywhistle or simply whistle.

Tune: A melody played by instruments. Not to be confused with a *song,* which consists of words set to a melody and sung by a human voice. Song, sung . . . get it?

Uilleann Pipes (pronounced "illin"): The Irish bagpipes, sweeter-sounding and wider in range than the more familiar Highland pipes. The wind for Irish pipes comes from a bellows rather than the mouth; that, combined with the fact that parts of the instrument stick out in all directions, requires that the player play in a sitting position. Nonetheless, it's not something you'd want to attempt while driving.

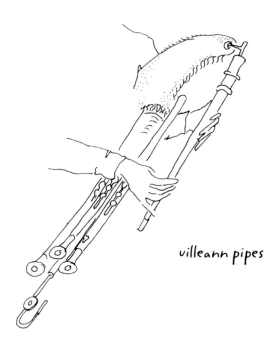

villeann pipes

CPSIA information can be obtained
at www.ICGtesting.com
Printed in the USA
FFOW03n1826060415
12402FF